Rural Praise

A parish workbook for worship in the country church

Rural Praise

A parish workbook for worship in the country church

Leslie J Francis

and

Jeremy Martineau

with illustrations by
Chris Bishop

First published in 1996

Gracewing
Fowler Wright Books
2 Southern Ave
Leominster
Herefordshire HR6 0QF

in association with
Acora Publishing
Arthur Rank Centre
Stoneleigh Park
Warwickshire CV8 2LZ

© Leslie J Francis and Jeremy Martineau, 1996
cartoons by Chris Bishop
Cover illustrations by Rafi Mohammed

ISBN 0 85244 388 9

Typesetting by Acora Publishing,
Stoneleigh Park, Warwickshire CV8 2LZ

Printed by Cromwell Press,
Broughton Gifford, Wiltshire SN12 8PH

Contents

Foreword

'Seven whole days, not one in seven, I will praise thee/In my heart, though not in heaven, I can raise thee.' So wrote one of the great saints of rural Anglicanism, the poet George Herbert, 'country parson' of the little church of Bemerton, just outside Salisbury. Herbert's words express well that centrality of the continuing praise of God which has always been one of the marks of the Church of England in its rural parishes particularly: throughout the countryside, our parish churches stand as reminders and reassurances to their communities that rural praise is being constantly offered.

Yet our situation is more complex than that in which George Herbert ministered and wrote. Our village societies are very different from the static, carefully ordered little community of Bemerton, with the church firmly at its centre. And our wider church life too, responding to the changes of society, shows a scene of great diversity. This workbook carefully presents some of the strands which make up that diversity in worship; it invites parishes to take note of people's expressed preferences, to reflect on the options available to them, and to engage in planned activities to help them discover how best God's praise may be offered in their own situation.

I commend this approach warmly to Parochial Church Councils and less formal church groups, to clergy, readers, churchwardens and all with responsibility for the planning of worship. There is a great deal of material in the following pages, and not all will be equally applicable to every church; but everyone, I am confident, will discover much of value for their own parish life of praise.

✠Thomas Leicester
Chair, Board of Mission
July 1996

Preface

This book reflects the two authors' firm commitment to and clear confidence in the rural church. We are convinced that planning for the future of the rural church needs both to be grounded in high quality research and to be rooted in local reflection and initiative. *Rural Praise* is a parish workbook which employs the findings of new research to help local churches reflect on their offering of worship to almighty God.

We wish to record our gratitude to those who have assisted us in preparing this book. First, the organisation of the research has involved many clergy and lay people throughout the rural dioceses of the Church of England. Without their help there could have been no book. Second, we acknowledge the significant role of the Principal and Governors of Trinity College, Carmarthen, in actively seeking to promote such research initiatives through the newly established Centre for Theology and Education. Third, we record our gratitude to Chris Bishop for enlivening and enriching our words and figures with such entertaining and thought-provoking illustrations. Finally, we record our gratitude to Andrea Osborn, Anne Rees and Diane Drayson who helped shape the manuscript, and to Katrina Terrance who prepared the camera ready copy.

Leslie J Francis
Trinity College Carmarthen

Jeremy Martineau
Arthur Rank Centre

August 1996

Introduction

Rural Praise is a parish workbook designed to help rural churches reflect on their offering of worship to almighty God.

There are thirty sections to this workbook. Some churches may decide to use them all. Other churches may wish to select a few examples. Some churches may decide to explore several sections at one time. Other churches may wish to spend longer over a smaller number of sections.

Each section has been drafted in the same way. First, key statistics are presented from a recent survey conducted among more than a thousand people who attend rural Anglican churches. Then a short reflection on these statistics is followed by questions for local study, and some suggested activities. These activities might well take place away from the normal place of worship, as well as within it.

The survey from which these statistics was taken asked rural churchgoers to rate how much different things contributed towards their experiences of good worship. The rating used a five point scale from *very negative*, through *neutral* to *very positive*.

Each set of statistics presents four pieces of key information. The pie chart distinguishes between the proportions of rural churchgoers who evaluate the issue as *positive, neutral* and *negative*. Then the statistics distinguish between the proportions of men and women who evaluate the issue as positive, and between the proportions of three age categories who evaluate the issue as positive: the under fifties, those between fifty and sixty-four, and those aged sixty-five and over. For example, the table presented in the first section on 'choosing the liturgy' shows that 24% of those under the age of fifty feel positive about the *Book of Common Prayer*, compared with 54% of those aged sixty-five or over.

Finally the statistics draw on psychological theory to distinguish between the views of extraverts and introverts (with ambiverts in between). Extraverts are people who like social gatherings and who prefer to act quickly. Introverts are people who prefer their own company and would rather think things through before acting. Since church congregations contain both introverts and extraverts, service planning should take the needs of both these orientations into account.

The questionnaire used to collect this information is printed in the appendix. Some churches may find it helpful to make copies of the questionnaire in order to compile a picture of how their churchgoers feel about these issues.

It is the writers' hope that discussion on these important issues will be carried out apart from the pressure to make policy decisions. Such discussions can then inform and advise those who need to take such decisions. It is to be expected that people will express support on those aspects with which they are most familiar. Churchgoers should recognise that some people may feel excluded if the pattern and style of services is too inflexible.

Suggestions on using this workbook

To plan a discussion on topics such as these, ensure that participants have the relevant background information in advance. The group may work best with between eight and ten people. To cover such a wide range of viewpoints will require experienced group leadership skills; the function of the group leader is to facilitate discussion, not to impose his or her own views. By modelling listening the leader will enable others to listen. It is important to allow space and time for sharing personal experiences which give rise to present opinions.

The aim of a discussion on any of these topics is to increase knowledge and awareness of some of the issues in rural worship. Sessions should not last more than ninety minutes. At the end of this time participants should have increased their knowledge concerning the breadth of possibilities and the ways in which worship can be enhanced. They should also be more aware of the origin and formation of their own views and those which others hold. They should have experienced differences as a positive contribution to life in the church.

It is often helpful for refreshments to be served on arrival. The leader or host should ensure that each person is known to everyone. To invite each person to say why they have come may be a useful way of opening the subject. It is more creative to use the time in different ways: working in twos or fours, by brainstorming ideas which are written on a flip chart, by using silence for a time of reflection, and only some time in plenary discussion. It is also important to recognise that extraverts feel much more at home with these group processes than introverts. It is important not to press introverts too hard into contributing in an extravert way. Such pressure may just force them to stay away.

1 Choosing the liturgy

Book of Common Prayer 1662

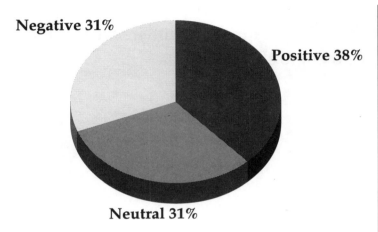

Positive 38%	
Males	40%
Females	38%
Under 50 years	24%
50-64 years	38%
Over 64 years	54%
Introverts	42%
Ambiverts	36%
Extraverts	39%

The Alternative Service Book 1980

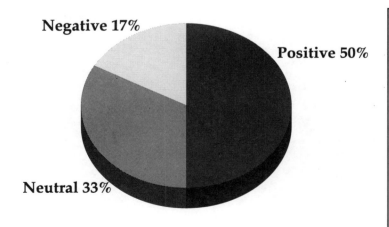

Positive 50%	
Males	50%
Females	51%
Under 50 years	56%
50-64 years	50%
Over 64 years	46%
Introverts	52%
Ambiverts	48%
Extraverts	52%

 **Listening to the statistics**

- More people have a positive view of *The Alternative Service Book 1980* than have a positive view of the *Book of Common Prayer 1662*.

- More people have a negative view of the *Book of Common Prayer 1662* than have a negative view of *The Alternative Service Book 1980*.

- Men and women hold very similar preferences between the *Book of Common Prayer 1662* and *The Alternative Service Book 1980*.

- Introverts and extraverts hold very similar preferences between the *Book of Common Prayer 1662* and *The Alternative Service Book 1980*.

- Age is the crucial determinant of preference for the *Book of Common Prayer 1662* or *The Alternative Service Book 1980*. Among those who are under fifty, 56% support *The Alternative Service Book 1980*, compared with 24% who support the *Book of Common Prayer 1662*. Among those who are sixty-five or over, 46% support *The Alternative Service Book 1980*, compared with 54% who support the *Book of Common Prayer 1662*.

Reflection

Liturgical change has been a slow and painful process for the Church of England. Two traditions now run side by side. While the new services seem to have captured the hearts of a younger generation of churchgoers, senior churchgoers remain more firmly committed to the traditional forms of services. How can rural churches respond best to this situation?

'Good-morning Madam, I represent the Royal Society for the Prevention of Cruelty to the Prayer Book....'

Activity

Make enlarged photocopies of the holy communion service from the *Book of Common Prayer* and from *The Alternative Service Book 1980* and create a display. Contrast the different styles of language. Illustrate the different sequences of the service components. Highlight the different emphases in theology.

Talking points

- When does your church use *The Alternative Service Book 1980*?

- When does your church use the *Book of Common Prayer 1662*?

- Does the choice of service book affect who comes?

- How important is the generation gap in your church on this issue?

- Should you try to help younger churchgoers appreciate the *Book of Common Prayer 1662*?

- Should you try to help senior churchgoers appreciate *The Alternative Service Book 1980*?

- How much do you expect your church to be using the *Book of Common Prayer 1662* in ten years time?

- Should we expect the language of worship to change over time to reflect changes in culture and everyday language?

2 Matins and evensong

Matins

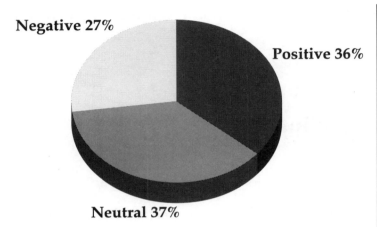

Positive 36%	
Males	35%
Females	37%
Under 50 years	27%
50-64 years	34%
Over 64 years	45%
Introverts	36%
Ambiverts	37%
Extraverts	34%

Evensong

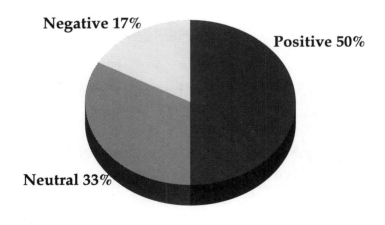

Positive 50%	
Males	50%
Females	52%
Under 50 years	48%
50-64 years	54%
Over 64 years	50%
Introverts	51%
Ambiverts	53%
Extraverts	48%

Listening to the statistics

- More people value evensong than value matins.

- Evensong is regarded positively by one in every two rural churchgoers.

- Matins is regarded positively by one in every three rural churchgoers.

- Men and women hold very similar views on matins and evensong.

- Evensong is just as popular among the under fifties as among the more senior churchgoers.

- Matins is much more popular among churchgoers aged sixty-five and over than among those under the age of fifty.

- Introverts and extraverts hold similar views about matins and evensong.

Reflection

Historically the Church of England has placed considerable emphasis on the offices of matins and evensong. Today these services appear much less popular than holy communion. Nevertheless, as many as 50% of rural churchgoers continue to find evensong an appropriate form of worship, and this percentage is holding up among the younger worshippers under the age of fifty. The situation is rather different, however, concerning matins. While there is almost as much support for matins as for evensong among churchgoers aged sixty-five and over, among those under the age of fifty support for matins drops considerably. The reduction in the numbers of priests can suggest greater frequency in matins, evensong and family services.

Activity

The offices of matins and evensong have their origin in the regular pattern of daily services conducted in the monasteries. Look at a complete set of these services and see how the pattern of canticles and prayers were structured to form a daily rhythm of prayer. Consider holding a parish workshop structured around saying these offices. The day could include a mixture of study (perhaps looking at a passage of scripture), work (perhaps spring cleaning the church and churchyard) and silent meditation.

Talking points

- How often does your church hold services of matins?

- How often does your church hold services of evensong?

- Who comes to matins and evensong in your church?

- Who is able to lead matins and evensong in your church when a priest is not available?

- How can the service of evensong be further promoted in your church?

- What gets in the way of more people attending evensong?

- What is the best time for evensong to begin?

3 Celebrating communion

Holy communion

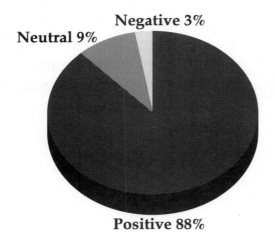

Negative 3%

Neutral 9%

Positive 88%

Positive 88%	
Males	88%
Females	87%
Under 50 years	85%
50-64 years	87%
Over 64 years	92%
Introverts	89%
Ambiverts	89%
Extraverts	86%

Sharing the peace

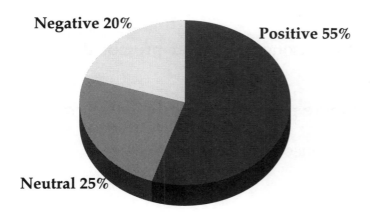

Negative 20%

Positive 55%

Neutral 25%

Positive 55%	
Males	56%
Females	54%
Under 50 years	60%
50-64 years	53%
Over 64 years	54%
Introverts	53%
Ambiverts	55%
Extraverts	58%

Listening to the statistics

- Rural churchgoers place a very high emphasis on holy communion.

- Holy communion is unimportant to only 3% of rural churchgoers.

- Men and women hold holy communion in equally high esteem.

- Introverts and extraverts hold very similar views on holy communion.

- Those who are under fifty are slightly (but only slightly) less eucharistically centred in their worship.

- More people support sharing the peace than disapprove of this practice.

- Men and women hold similar views on sharing the peace.

- Those who are aged fifty and over are slightly less positive about sharing the peace.

- Introverts are slightly less comfortable than extraverts about sharing the peace.

Reflection

The communion service is now clearly central to what it means to be an Anglican within the rural community. Currently, however, two related trends make it increasingly difficult for the rural church to provide communion services. Overall there are fewer priests working in rural dioceses than in an earlier generation. The priests who remain in rural areas are now responsible for more and more churches. One solution is to ordain local people to preside at the eucharist. Another solution is to encourage 'communion by extension', where lay people are authorised to structure and lead the communion service using bread and wine consecrated on a previous occasion or in another church.

Activity

Arrange a visit to a church where communion is celebrated in a very different way from within your own church. This could be to another Anglican church of very different churchmanship, or to a church of a different denomination. Then create a poster display noting the similarities and differences compared with your own church, and your reactions to this different way of doing things.

Talking points

- Is communion celebrated often enough or too often in your church?

- Is the sacrament reserved in your church?

- Is 'communion by extension' practised in your church?

- How do you feel about a communion service led by a lay person (for example, a reader), using bread and wine consecrated at a previous service or in another church?

- Has the Church of England placed too much emphasis on holy communion?

- Is the peace shared in your church? What is its significance?

- Does sharing the peace make some of your congregation feel uncomfortable?

- Why do some people find sharing the peace a positive experience and others find it a negative experience?

4 Positioning the altar

Clergy facing the people

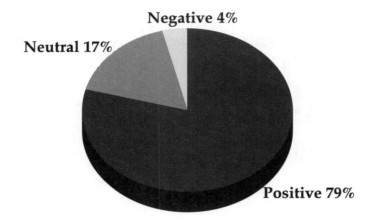

Positive 79%	
Males	77%
Females	80%
Under 50 years	80%
50-64 years	75%
Over 64 years	81%
Introverts	81%
Ambiverts	76%
Extraverts	78%

Clergy facing the altar

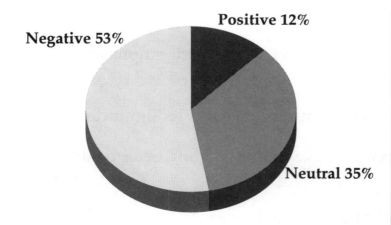

Positive 12%	
Males	11%
Females	13%
Under 50 years	11%
50-64 years	14%
Over 64 years	11%
Introverts	13%
Ambiverts	12%
Extraverts	10%

 **Listening to the statistics**

- Many more churchgoers are in favour of the clergy facing the people than are in favour of the clergy facing away from the people.

- Only 4% of churchgoers feel that clergy facing the people is a negative experience, while 53% of them feel that clergy facing away from the people is a negative experience.

- Men and women hold very similar views about the direction in which the clergy face.

- Age makes very little difference to how people feel about the direction in which the clergy face.

- Introverts and extraverts are equally committed to the view that the clergy should face the people.

Reflection

The majority of rural churches are either medieval or built during the Victorian period to look like medieval churches. Medieval churches were designed to focus attention on the altar (usually at the east end) where the priest presided with his back to the people. This architectural style reflected *theological* views about the mystery of the eucharist and about the role of the priest. Modern liturgy reflects a different theology of the eucharist and emphasises the role of the whole congregation in the celebration. While the majority of churchgoers now seem to accept the practical consequence of the change, often the architecture of the rural church makes it difficult to reposition the altar.

Well Reverend, this is THE new all
moveable communion table as
produced by us at Altar-Native Liturgies Ltd.

Activity

Reorder your church building as much as possible to arrange a eucharist using the altar position with which you are least familiar. If you are used to seeing the altar at the far end of the chancel, move the pews to try out a nave altar. If you are used to a nave altar, hold a service using an altar at the far end of the chancel with the priest facing away from the people. After the service discuss your thoughts and feelings.

Talking points

•   What is said about the eucharist, about priesthood and about God when the altar is at the far end of the church and the priest faces away from the people?

•   What is said about the eucharist, about priesthood and about God when the altar is in the nave and the priest faces the people?

•   Where is the altar positioned in your church?

•   What does the architecture of your church say about the eucharist and about the roles of the priest and the people?

•   If you could design a church from scratch, where would you place the altar?

•   Is the altar in the best place in your church?

5 Structuring family services

Family services

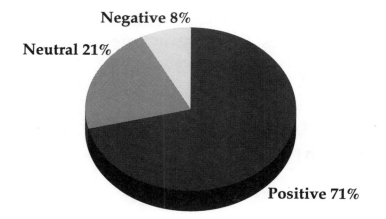

Positive 71%	
Males	71%
Females	72%
Under 50 years	81%
50-64 years	65%
Over 64 years	68%
Introverts	72%
Ambiverts	71%
Extraverts	70%

Informal services

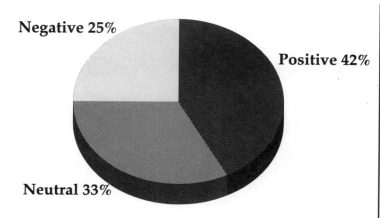

Positive 42%	
Males	38%
Females	46%
Under 50 years	56%
50-64 years	39%
Over 64 years	33%
Introverts	42%
Ambiverts	44%
Extraverts	42%

Listening to the statistics

- Seven out of ten churchgoers support the idea of family services.

- Family services are supported equally by men and by women.

- Family services are supported equally by introverts and extraverts.

- While family services receive most support from the under fifties, they are still supported by as many as two out of every three more senior churchgoers.

- There is much less support for informal services than for family services.

- Men show less support than women for informal services.

- Senior churchgoers show less support than younger churchgoers for informal services.

- Introverts and extraverts show an equal level of support for informal services.

Reflection

Family services have developed in frequency and popularity during the past two decades. This one name, however, includes a number of different expressions. Some family services in fact follow a recognised eucharistic rite. Some family services follow a regular structure based on morning prayer, the CPAS order of family worship, or the publication *Come and Worship*. Other family services follow a much less structured pattern and reflect a Free Church tradition more than an Anglican tradition. The statistics show considerable goodwill among rural churchgoers for family services, but this goodwill seems to be more directed to the kind of family service which follows a formal structure than to the kind of family service which is more informal.

Activity

Examine several different frameworks for family services. For example look at the CPAS order of family worship, or the publication *Come and Worship*. Invite a diocesan adviser to come to speak about different ways of holding family services. Arrange to hold a family service along different lines from those normally held in your church. Make a special effort to invite people to this service. Then evaluate the contribution of this service to the life of your church.

Talking points

- How often does your church hold a family service?

- What does your church mean by a family service?

- What are the advantages of family services following a formal structure?

- What are the advantages of family services following an informal structure?

- Who comes to the family service?

- Does the family service meet a need not met by other services?

- How would you like to modify or improve family services in your church?

- Who is (or could be) involved in leading family services in your church?

- What skills are required for leading these services?

6 Services of hymns and readings

Songs of praise services

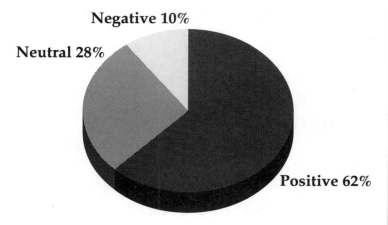

Positive 62%	
Males	62%
Females	62%
Under 50 years	65%
50-64 years	62%
Over 64 years	59%
Introverts	63%
Ambiverts	63%
Extraverts	59%

Readings from non biblical books

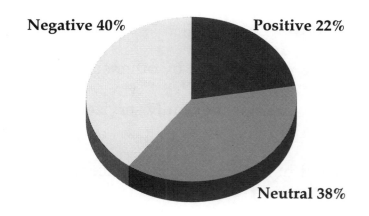

Positive 22%	
Males	19%
Females	25%
Under 50 years	33%
50-64 years	20%
Over 64 years	14%
Introverts	20%
Ambiverts	22%
Extraverts	23%

Listening to the statistics

- Songs of praise services receive support from six out of ten regular churchgoers.

- Men and women are equally supportive of songs of praise services.

- Senior churchgoers are slightly less supportive of songs of praise services than younger churchgoers.

- There is little difference in the support given to songs of praise services by introverts and extraverts.

- While the majority of rural churchgoers support services like songs of praise, they are much less likely to support the use of non biblical readings in such services.

- Men are less likely than women to appreciate readings from non biblical books.

- Churchgoers under the age of fifty are twice as likely as churchgoers over the age of sixty-four to appreciate readings from non biblical books.

- Introverts and extraverts show similar kinds of appreciation for readings from non biblical books.

Reflection

Songs of praise is a form of worship made popular through television. Many churches structure services on this model on either a regular or an occasional basis. These services are based around a selection of hymns and many include readings from scripture, personal stories or testimonies, short homilies and secular materials. The statistics show that there is considerable support for songs of praise services within the rural church. At the same time the statistics suggest that there may be a preference for traditional religious materials rather than readings from non biblical books. A key challenge remains in developing the best potential for these services.

Activity

Hold a workshop to plan a service which makes full use of readings from non biblical books. Set an appropriate theme which lends itself to resourcing from non biblical material. Examples might include *water* (giving thanks for baptism), *spring* (giving thanks for new life) and *food* (giving thanks for the harvest). Prepare for the workshop by assembling a set of books, including anthologies, and by inviting participants to bring their own materials. Appropriate material should be available from your diocesan resource centre.

Talking points

- How often are songs of praise services held in your church?

- Who leads songs of praise services in your church, and who else contributes (or could contribute) to the leadership?

- How are the hymns chosen for songs of praise services in your church?

- Who comes to songs of praise services who tends not to come to other services?

- How can songs of praise services be improved or enhanced in your church?

- How are (or can) readings for non biblical books be best used in your church?

7 Choosing hymns

Modern hymns

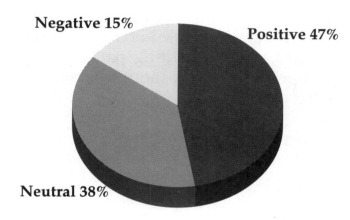

Positive 47%	
Males	46%
Females	49%
Under 50 years	58%
50-64 years	44%
Over 64 years	42%
Introverts	47%
Ambiverts	49%
Extraverts	49%

Traditional hymns

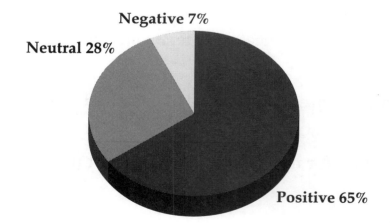

Positive 65%	
Males	65%
Females	63%
Under 50 years	55%
50-64 years	64%
Over 64 years	72%
Introverts	69%
Ambiverts	61%
Extraverts	63%

 **Listening to the statistics**

- A higher proportion of rural churchgoers welcome traditional hymns than welcome modern hymns.

- Twice as many rural churchgoers feel negatively about modern hymns than feel negatively about traditional hymns.

- Men and women hold quite similar preferences regarding traditional hymns.

- Introverts are slightly more inclined than extraverts to emphasise a preference for traditional hymns.

- Preferences for modern and traditional hymns is clearly related to age.

- Churchgoers under the age of fifty display a considerably stronger liking for modern hymns.

- Churchgoers over the age of sixty-four display a considerably stronger liking for traditional hymns.

Reflection

Singing plays an important part in many church services. The choice of hymns, therefore, makes a big contribution to the way in which individual worshippers feel about the whole service. A number of issues have to be taken into account when choosing hymns. Do the hymns reflect the theme of the service? Are the hymns known? Are the tunes singable? Can the organist play these tunes? Are the tunes too high or too low for the usual congregation to sing? In addition to these considerations, hymns reflect different generations. The hymns children learn to sing from books like *Come and Praise* are often quite different from the hymns in the more traditional hymnbooks used in churches.

The choice of hymns: method 1

Activity

Ask the local primary school if they would be willing to invite a group from the church to attend one of their special assemblies when the children are singing a set of their modern school hymns. Find out what the hymns are beforehand and try to learn them. The school hymn book *Come and Praise* is supported by a series of audio cassettes.

Talking points

- How important are hymns to the services in your church?

- How well are the hymns generally known?

- How well are the hymns generally sung?

- Who usually chooses the hymns?

- How well do children from the local school know the hymns used in your church?

- How willing is your congregation to learn new hymns?

- How important do you think it is to learn new hymns?

- Why are some people so resistant to learning new hymns?

8 Choruses and songs

Choruses

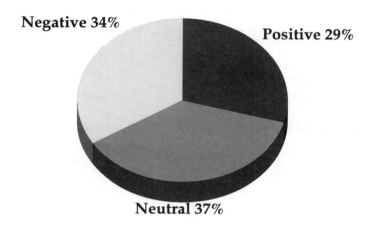

Negative 34% Positive 29%

Neutral 37%

Positive 29%	
Males	28%
Females	31%
Under 50 years	39%
50-64 years	30%
Over 64 years	20%
Introverts	25%
Ambiverts	31%
Extraverts	33%

Gospel songs

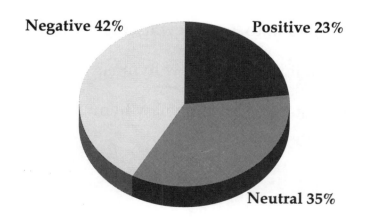

Negative 42% Positive 23%

Neutral 35%

Positive 23%	
Males	22%
Females	25%
Under 50 years	35%
50-64 years	22%
Over 64 years	13%
Introverts	22%
Ambiverts	23%
Extraverts	26%

Listening to the statistics

- The majority of rural churchgoers do not appreciate singing choruses and gospel songs.

- Nearly twice as many rural churchgoers feel that gospel songs make a negative contribution to worship as feel that they make a positive contribution to worship.

- Men and women hold similar attitudes to choruses and gospel songs.

- Extraverts are more likely to appreciate choruses than introverts.

- People under the age of fifty are twice as likely to appreciate choruses than people over the age of sixty-five.

- People under the age of fifty are nearly three times as likely to appreciate gospel songs as people over the age of sixty-five.

Reflection

Choruses and gospel songs have been made more widely available in rural churches through books like *Mission Praise*. Songs of this nature are often thought to appeal to people on the fringes of the church and to make the worship of the local church more accessible. The statistics make it clear, however, that the more established churchgoers have been slow to adjust to this idiom. While this form of music is more acceptable to the younger group of churchgoers than to the older group, it has to be recognised that even among the under fifty year olds, fewer than two in five find choruses and gospel songs conducive to good worship.

Activity

Discover which churches and chapels in the area use choruses. Attend one of these services to participate in the worship. Afterwards discuss your feelings about attending this type of worship.

Talking points

• How much use does your church make of choruses and gospel songs?

• When does your church make use of choruses and gospel songs?

• How well are choruses and gospel songs appreciated in your church?

• What are the advantages of using choruses and gospel songs?

• What are the disadvantages of using choruses and gospel songs?

• Why are younger churchgoers more likely to appreciate choruses and gospel songs?

9 Planning the books

Enough bibles for everyone

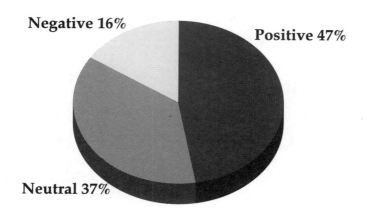

Positive 47%	
Males	51%
Females	45%
Under 50 years	52%
50-64 years	46%
Over 64 years	46%
Introverts	47%
Ambiverts	46%
Extraverts	51%

Books in good condition

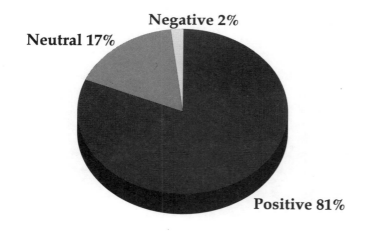

Positive 81%	
Males	83%
Females	78%
Under 50 years	72%
50-64 years	81%
Over 64 years	88%
Introverts	83%
Ambiverts	83%
Extraverts	75%

 # Listening to the statistics

- The majority of churchgoers feel that it is important for the hymnbooks and service books to be in good condition.

- Men are slightly more concerned about the condition of the books than women.

- Introverts are a little more concerned about the condition of the books than extraverts.

- Senior churchgoers are more concerned about the condition of the books than churchgoers under the age of fifty.

- Almost half the rural churchgoers feel that it is important for there to be enough pew bibles.

- Men are slightly more concerned than women that there should be enough pew bibles.

- Extraverts are slightly more concerned about the provision of pew bibles than introverts.

- Churchgoers under the age of fifty are more concerned about the provision of pew bibles than senior churchgoers.

Reflection

Books are often of central importance in Anglican churches. People need service books to follow the service and to take a full part. People need hymnbooks to take part in the singing. Many churches also provide copies of the bible for people to follow the readings or to use during the sermon. Books may be particularly important for visitors and may help to shape the attitudes of newcomers to the church. In some churches there are insufficient books to go round. Some churches continue to use books which are in poor condition or have pages missing.

Welcome to St Enid's.
These are the books you will need
for the service this morning.

Activity

Visit a number of local churches (of various denominations) and take a careful look at the availability of service books, hymn books and pew bibles. Then discuss your impressions on what you have found. What do the books say about the local church?

Talking points

• What books are available in your church?

• In what condition are the books in your church?

• Are there enough books to go round at the major services, like Christmas?

• Does anything need to be done to improve the quality of the books?

• Does your church have a set of pew bibles?

• What are the advantages of pew bibles?

• What are the disadvantages of pew bibles?

• Who is responsible for making sure that visitors and newcomers have the right books?

10   Caring for children

Children present for the service

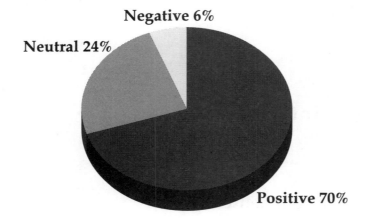

Positive 70%	
Males	69%
Females	71%
Under 50 years	77%
50-64 years	65%
Over 64 years	69%
Introverts	68%
Ambiverts	71%
Extraverts	72%

Crèche facilities

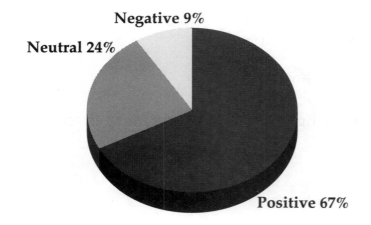

Positive 67%	
Males	67%
Females	67%
Under 50 years	67%
50-64 years	66%
Over 64 years	69%
Introverts	65%
Ambiverts	67%
Extraverts	68%

 **Listening to the statistics**

- The majority of rural churchgoers appreciate children being present for the service.

- Only 6% of rural churchgoers feel that the presence of children has a negative impact on worship.

- Extraverts have a slightly more welcoming attitude to children than introverts.

- Churchgoers under the age of fifty have a more welcoming attitude to children than more senior churchgoers.

- The majority of rural churchgoers recognise the importance of crèche facilities.

- Introverts and extraverts show equal support for crèche facilities.

- Younger and more senior churchgoers show equal support for crèche facilities.

- Men and women are equally welcoming of children in church and of the provision of crèche facilities.

Reflection

In a number of church reports emphasis has been placed on the importance of welcoming children as part of the church congregation. This emphasis is present in *The Child in the Church* (1976) and *Children in the Way* (1988). With the demise of Sunday schools, the church service has become the main point of contact between children and Christian teaching. The statistics show that the majority of rural churchgoers now welcome the presence of children at services, although this welcome is still a little stronger among the younger churchgoers. The majority of churchgoers also recognise the importance of the provision of crèche facilities for young children. When adults are invited to work among children in your church, seek advice from the diocesan children's adviser about issues like vetting procedures, insurance and training opportunities.

Activity

Take a major church report on ministry among children, like *Children in the Way*, and arrange a study session on it. Consider inviting the diocesan children's adviser to help with the session. Work out the implications of this report for life in your own church, including the appropriate budget for resourcing work with children, providing accessible advice for parents who wish to involve their children in the life of the church, and for developing a church policy for children.

Talking points

•   How many children are present at services in your church?

•   What is done to help children feel welcome at services in your church?

•   Can (or should) more be done to help children feel at home in church?

•   Who helps (or can help) with ministry among children in your church?

•   Are crèche facilities available in your church (or should they be)?

•   Are proper vetting procedures employed before engaging people to work with children?

•   Are proper training opportunities offered to people working with children in your church?

11   Using the scriptures

Traditional bible translations

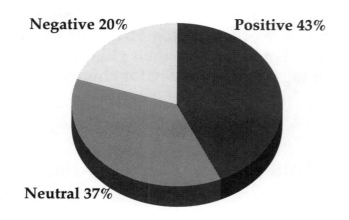

	Positive 43%	
Males		42%
Females		43%
Under 50 years		28%
50-64 years		46%
Over 64 years		53%
Introverts		45%
Ambiverts		42%
Extraverts		40%

Modern bible translations

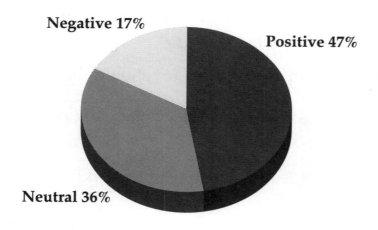

	Positive 47%	
Males		48%
Females		46%
Under 50 years		55%
50-64 years		46%
Over 64 years		41%
Introverts		49%
Ambiverts		47%
Extraverts		46%

 # Listening to the statistics

- Rural churchgoers are almost evenly split on their preference for traditional and modern translations of the bible.

- One in five churchgoers say that they feel traditional bible translations unhelpful.

- Almost one in five churchgoers say that they feel modern bible translations unhelpful.

- Men and women hold similar preferences for traditional and modern bible translations.

- Introverts show a slightly greater tendency than extraverts to prefer traditional bible translations.

- Churchgoers over the age of sixty-four show twice as much support for traditional bible translation compared with churchgoers under the age of fifty.

- Younger churchgoers are more inclined to prefer modern bible translations than senior churchgoers.

Reflection

Until the 1960s the majority of Anglican churches remained faithful to the *Authorised Version* of scripture. More recent translations set out to offer a more accurate translation of the original Hebrew or Greek, or to communicate more clearly in contemporary language. Some of the most recent translations have taken on board the issue of inclusive language. By selecting readings from a number of different translations of scripture, *The Alternative Service Book 1980* demonstrated that the Church of England was unwilling to promote any one specific modern translation of scripture. The other major change in the use of scripture in church concerns the wider range of people involved as readers.

'And they removed from the desert of Sinai,
and pitched at Kibroth-hattaavah.
And they departed from Kibroth-hattaavah,
and encamped at Hazeroth, and they departed....'

Activity

Collect as many different translations of scripture as you can. Select a few well chosen passages and compare different translations. It may be a good idea to take on a passage well known for its poetry in the *Authorised Version* (for example the opening of John's gospel) and another passage which displays concentrated argument (like Paul's letter to the Romans). Listen to the various translations read aloud and also compare the texts set out side by side.

Talking points

• Who reads the scriptures in your church service?

• Who decides which versions of scripture will be used in your church?

• Are you aware of individual preferences for different versions of scripture in your church?

• Are there other people who can (or should) be involved as lesson readers in your church?

• What training is offered for lesson readers in your church?

• Are men and women, children and adults given equal opportunities to read lessons (or should they be)?

• What is your view on choosing an inclusive language version of scripture?

12   Using the architecture

Traditional church architecture

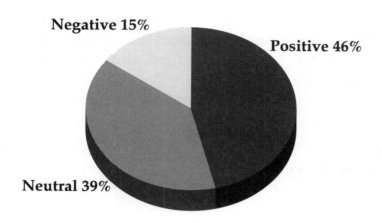

Negative 15%
Positive 46%
Neutral 39%

Positive 46%	
Males	45%
Females	46%
Under 50 years	38%
50-64 years	46%
Over 64 years	53%
Introverts	42%
Ambiverts	46%
Extraverts	49%

Modern church building

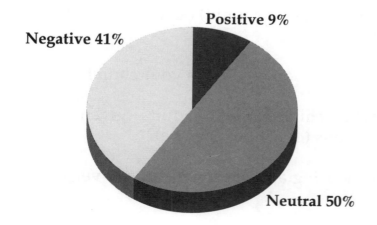

Positive 9%
Negative 41%
Neutral 50%

Positive 9%	
Males	12%
Females	6%
Under 50 years	8%
50-64 years	10%
Over 64 years	9%
Introverts	8%
Ambiverts	10%
Extraverts	8%

Listening to the statistics

- Very few rural churchgoers feel their worship is enhanced by modern church buildings.

- Two in five rural churchgoers feel that modern church architecture has a negative impact on their sense of worship.

- Slightly fewer than half of rural churchgoers feel their worship is enhanced by traditional church architecture.

- Men and women hold similar views on traditional church architecture.

- Men are more open than women to modern church architecture.

- Introverts are slightly more committed to traditional church architecture than extraverts.

- Churchgoers over the age of sixty-four are more committed to traditional church architecture than churchgoers under the age of fifty.

Reflection

The rural church invests a great deal of energy and finance in maintaining medieval and neo medieval churches. There are two key arguments for continuing to use these churches. They are thought to be important symbols of the presence of the church in rural communities. They are thought to provide an important focus and stimulus for worship among those who attend services. The statistics show that for just over half of rural churchgoers traditional church architecture is either irrelevant or a distraction. On the other hand, rural churchgoers show very little enthusiasm for modern church architecture. There is much interest in using part of churches for activities other than worship. How can this be achieved without adversely affecting the church as a 'Holy Place'?

Activity

Find out where there are examples of modern church architecture in your area and arrange a visit to some of these places. Give particular attention to the new Roman Catholic churches which have been built to serve rural areas. See, too, how old buildings have been transformed by modern additions and adaptations. Find out the range of uses for which the parts of the church building have been put over the years.

Talking points

- How would you describe the architecture of your church?

- How much does it cost to maintain your church building?

- How important is the church building to the local community?

- How important is the church building to those who worship there?

- How can (or should) the architecture of your church best be used to enrich worship?

- Are there ways in which the building can (or should) be adapted to enrich worship?

- Can the church be of greater use to the community in addition to being a place of worship?

13   Using the space

Congregation spread out

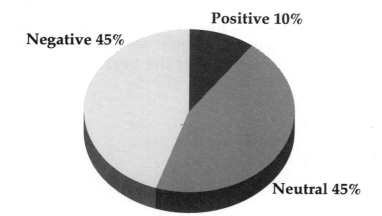

Positive 10%	
Males	11%
Females	9%
Under 50 years	5%
50-64 years	11%
Over 64 years	14%
Introverts	7%
Ambiverts	11%
Extraverts	10%

Congregation seated together

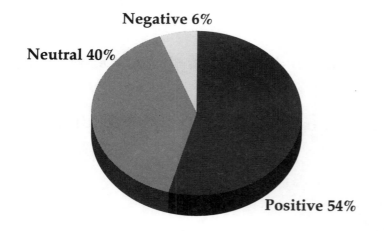

Positive 54%	
Males	54%
Females	54%
Under 50 years	57%
50-64 years	52%
Over 64 years	54%
Introverts	49%
Ambiverts	57%
Extraverts	56%

Listening to the statistics

- Rural churchgoers can see much more advantage in the congregation sitting together than being spread out over the church.

- Only 6% of rural churchgoers see disadvantages in the congregation being seated together, compared with 45% who see disadvantages in the congregation being spread out.

- Men and women have similar views about the advantages of the congregation seated together.

- Senior churchgoers are slightly more likely than younger churchgoers to prefer the congregation spread out.

- Introverts are a little less likely than extraverts to see the advantages of the congregation seated together.

Reflection

Many rural churches are provided with fixed seating or pews designed to accommodate many more people than those who attend the usual Sunday services. Quite often a small congregation is spread out throughout a large building. Sometimes there are historic reasons for this, since certain families have always tended to occupy the same pew. Sometimes there are social reasons for this, since certain individuals are reluctant to mix with each other. Sometimes there are personal reasons for this, since certain individuals actually need the feeling of space and value being separated from other worshippers. Because of all these reasons, changing the seating arrangements in the rural church can be controversial.

During the singing of the second hymn we will ALL enjoy a liturgical game of musical pews!

Activity

Design an act of worship during which people are invited to change their position in the church, to move from one seat to another. Begin the service with people sitting in their usual places. At the opening of the service invite them to experience the sense of being alone with God and to choose a place in the church as far away as possible from other people. Then look at the next stage of the service, invite them to share the peace, to experience the fellowship of the people of God and to sit together in a group.

Talking points

- How many people generally attend your church?

- How many people can sit comfortably in your church?

- When are all the seats filled to capacity?

- Where do the regular worshippers sit and is there a pattern to this?

- Do you feel that the best use is made of seating in your church?

- Have attempts been made to change the seating pattern?

- Do you think that any change is needed?

14   Designing the seating

Traditional pews

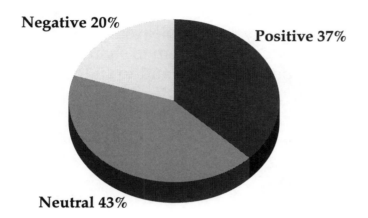

Positive 37%	
Males	37%
Females	38%
Under 50 years	32%
50-64 years	38%
Over 64 years	42%
Introverts	38%
Ambiverts	36%
Extraverts	38%

Modern chairs

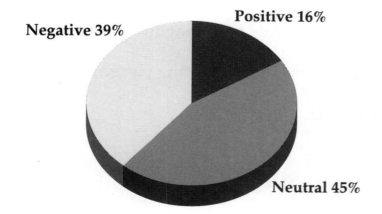

Positive 16%	
Males	21%
Females	13%
Under 50 years	18%
50-64 years	16%
Over 64 years	15%
Introverts	17%
Ambiverts	15%
Extraverts	18%

 **Listening to the statistics**

- Nearly half of rural churchgoers are unconcerned whether churches have traditional pews or modern chairs.

- Two out of every five churchgoers are against modern chairs while one out of every five is against traditional pews.

- Twice as many churchgoers claim to find positive advantages in traditional pews compared with those who find positive advantages in modern chairs.

- Men are slightly more inclined to favour modern chairs than women.

- Introverts and extraverts hold similar views about the comparative advantages of traditional pews and modern chairs.

- Senior churchgoers show more attachment to the traditional pews than younger churchgoers.

Reflection

Taste in church furnishings have changed many times over the centuries. Many medieval churches may have kept much of the nave free from seating, apart from around the walls. In the seventeenth century the fashion was for box pews with high sides, and each with its own door. In the Victorian period many churches were equipped with more open pine pews. Today some churches prefer the flexibility of chairs which can be rearranged according to changing needs. A small regular congregation can be comfortably accommodated around the altar. For large carol services and funerals, the maximum seating potential of the building can be fully exploited. On special occasions, all the chairs can be cleared from the centre for drama, musical presentations, or even the harvest supper.

We thought
we would rearrange
the seating for
the Confirmation service

Activity

If at all possible experiment with moving the seating in your church. See how different seating arrangements proclaim different messages about your church and about your worship. It might be possible to consider different forms of seating in a side chapel, at the back of the nave or in an aisle to facilitate small group worship, discussion groups, or other forms of activity.

Talking points

- What kind of seating is provided in your church?

- When was this seating installed?

- What kind of seating did the current system replace?

- How comfortable are the seats in your church?

- What are the main advantages of the seats in your church?

- What are the main disadvantages of the seats in your church?

- In what ways could the church be used differently if there was a different form of seating?

- What do you imagine the seating will be like in your church in fifty years time?

15   Considering the disabled

Access for the disabled

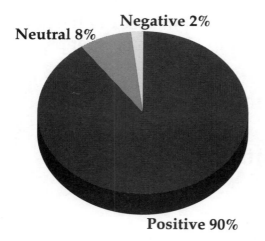

Positive 90%	
Males	90%
Females	91%
Under 50 years	91%
50-64 years	88%
Over 64 years	92%
Introverts	93%
Ambiverts	89%
Extraverts	90%

Loop system for the hard-of-hearing

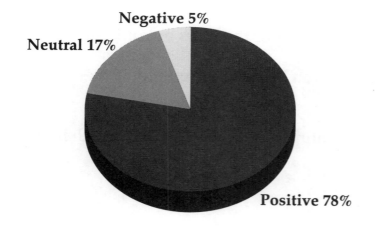

Positive 78%	
Males	77%
Females	80%
Under 50 years	77%
50-64 years	78%
Over 64 years	81%
Introverts	78%
Ambiverts	79%
Extraverts	79%

 **Listening to the statistics**

- Nine out of ten churchgoers are convinced by the need for access for disabled people.

- Eight out of ten churchgoers are convinced by the need for a loop system for the hard-of-hearing.

- Men and women hold similar views on the needs of disabled people and those who are hard-of-hearing.

- Introverts and extraverts hold similar views on the needs of disabled people and those who are hard-of-hearing.

- Younger and senior churchgoers hold similar views on the needs of disabled people and those who are hard-of-hearing.

Reflection

Many churches were built in an age when the special needs of disabled people were not taken carefully into account. In some churches the steps up to or down from the porch and main entrance may make wheelchair access difficult and entry hazardous for the infirm. In some churches the sheer size of the building and the position of altar, lectern and pulpit may make things particularly difficult for the deaf and hard-of-hearing. There may be particular hazards for visually impaired people. The path from the pews to the altar rail for distribution of communion may involve negotiating steps (without handrails), avoiding sharp edged furniture and traversing uneven floors. Considerable modification in the design or *use* of a church may become necessary to make the building really hospitable, welcoming and safe for disabled people. (Is there clear visibility of those who will be speaking? In what ways might the needs of those with learning difficulties be met?)

Welcome to the Parish Church
of St Simeon the Inaccessible

Activity

Explore your church from the perspective of individuals suffering from various disabilities. For example, borrow a wheelchair to explore ease of access to various parts of the church building. Try to find your way to the altar rail blindfolded and note the hazards in the way. Check the visibility of the hymn books for the visually impaired. Check the audibility of speech from the pulpit, lectern, altar and other key points in the church. Find out what grants may be available from the local council or trusts to provide for the needs of disabled people.

Talking points

- How many physically disabled people attend your church?

- How many visually impaired people attend your church?

- How many hard-of-hearing people attend your church?

- How many people with learning difficulties attend your church?

- What particular difficulties do the physically disabled confront in your church?

- What particular difficulties do the visually impaired confront in your church?

- What particular difficulties do the hard-of-hearing confront in your church?

- What particular difficulties do those with learning difficulties confront in your church?

- What more can or should your church do to consider the needs of people who are variously disabled?

16   Light and sound

Good lighting system

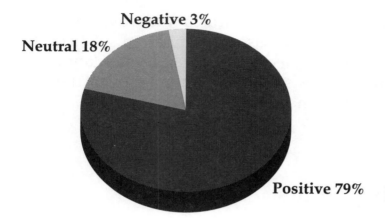

Positive 79%	
Males	80%
Females	79%
Under 50 years	67%
50-64 years	80%
Over 64 years	91%
Introverts	82%
Ambiverts	81%
Extraverts	76%

Good sound system

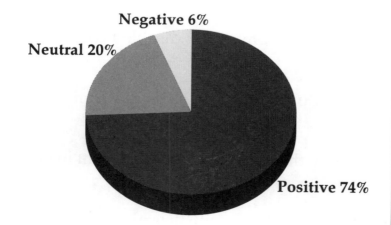

Positive 74%	
Males	73%
Females	74%
Under 50 years	66%
50-64 years	73%
Over 64 years	81%
Introverts	77%
Ambiverts	76%
Extraverts	69%

Listening to the statistics

- A good lighting system is important to four out of every five churchgoers.

- A good sound system is important to three out of every four churchgoers.

- Three churchgoers in a hundred feel that a good lighting system is inimical to the right atmosphere for worship.

- Six churchgoers in a hundred feel that a good sound system is inimical to the right atmosphere for worship.

- Introverts are more likely than extraverts to value a good lighting system and a good sound system.

- Senior churchgoers are more likely than younger churchgoers to value a good lighting system and a good sound system.

- Men and women hold similar views on lighting systems and on sound systems.

Reflection

Throughout the medieval period, from the Saxon period to the high Gothic style of the early sixteenth century, church windows grew from very small openings to huge arched lights. Many were filled with stained glass. The Gothic revival imitated earlier styles without particular concern for the amount of natural light let into the church itself. As a consequence the provision of a good lighting system within a church requires careful tailoring to the specific needs of individual buildings. Good lighting needs to respect the atmosphere of the building as well as meet the practical needs of the worshippers. In a similar way good sound systems generally need to be tailor made, taking into account the architecture of the building, the natural acoustics and the ways in which the building is generally used in services and on other occasions.

The new standard stereo speakers, specially designed to blend with your architecture. Also available in chunky Norman or delicate Perpendicular

Activity

Go into the church after dark and take a careful look at the lighting system. What does the lighting system look like? How well does the lighting system blend into the whole environment of the church? How efficient and how effective is the lighting system? Try reading the small print of the service books at different parts of the church.

Talking points

- Does your church have a lighting system?

- When was the current lighting system installed in your church?

- How adequate is the lighting system in your church?

- Does the lighting system need modification and, if so, how?

- Does your church have a sound system?

- When was the current sound system installed in your church?

- How adequate is the sound system in your church?

- Does the sound system need modification and, if so, how?

- Would a sound system which included the capability of playing cassettes and CDs be a benefit?

- Does the Diocesan Advisory Committee have a technical adviser on sound/lighting?

17   Human comfort

Good heating system

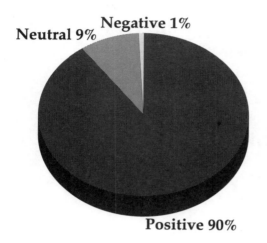

Positive 90%	
Males	89%
Females	90%
Under 50 years	85%
50-64 years	90%
Over 64 years	94%
Introverts	92%
Ambiverts	91%
Extraverts	87%

Toilet available

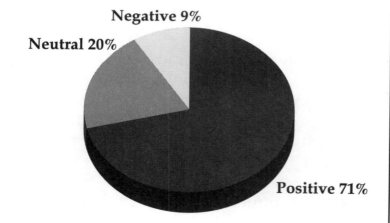

Positive 71%	
Males	71%
Females	72%
Under 50 years	72%
50-64 years	68%
Over 64 years	76%
Introverts	75%
Ambiverts	73%
Extraverts	69%

Listening to the statistics

- The vast majority of churchgoers (90%) feel that a good heating system is important in the local church.

- Only one in a hundred worshippers feel that a warm church spoils their sense of worship.

- Senior churchgoers value a good heating system more than younger churchgoers.

- Introverts value a good heating system more than extraverts.

- Seven out of ten churchgoers feel that it is important for a toilet to be available at church.

- Both senior churchgoers and younger churchgoers (who have children) give more importance to a toilet at church than the middle age group.

- Introverts give more importance to a toilet at church than extraverts.

- Men and women hold similar attitudes toward human comfort at church.

Reflection

The majority of rural churches were built in an age which held very different concepts of human comfort from those shared in our current society. There is nothing particularly religious or virtuous, however, in being cold or deprived of toilet facilities. One of the major tensions faced by rural churches today is the conflict between keeping the ancient church building in the original form and adapting it to serve the needs of the local worshipping community. Conservation and aesthetics on the one hand come into conflict with practicality and relevance on the other hand. If expense prevents a whole building being properly heated, it may be possible to devise ways of heating part of it. Redesigning the interior of the nave, porch or tower may find suitable locations for kitchens and toilets. Such adaptations, however, need to be protected from frosts and adequately cleaned and maintained. Many people feel uneasy about not having easy access to a toilet.

At our church the Easter Eve Service and the lighting of the Easter Fire is a very popular service.

That's only because it's the warmest the church ever gets

Activity

Discover where local churches have been developed to make a more efficient and more economical use of heating during winter. Visit these churches. Compare the heating systems in several local churches.

Talking points

- How is your church heated?

- When was the heating system designed?

- How effective and how efficient is the heating system?

- How much does the heating system cost to run?

- Do people stay away from church because of the cold?

- Are there ways in which the building could be adapted to improve heating in winter?

- Is there a toilet available at church?

- When was the toilet installed and is it adequate?

- Are new toilet facilities needed?

- Is any overall plan needed for improving human comfort in your church?

18   Using silence

Periods for silence

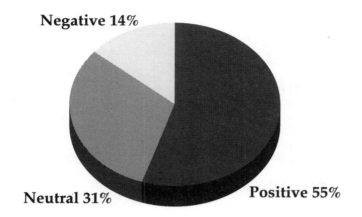

	Positive 55%
Males	53%
Females	57%
Under 50 years	60%
50-64 years	56%
Over 64 years	50%
Introverts	48%
Ambiverts	60%
Extraverts	56%

Silence before the service

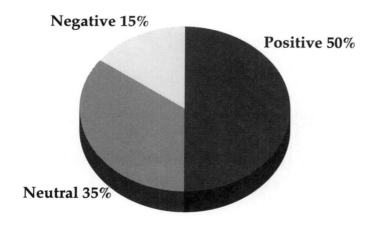

	Positive 50%
Males	50%
Females	50%
Under 50 years	39%
50-64 years	54%
Over 64 years	55%
Introverts	50%
Ambiverts	53%
Extraverts	48%

 **Listening to the statistics**

- Many more rural churchgoers value silence in church than reject silence.

- Half of rural churchgoers value silence before the service while only 15% do not.

- More than half of rural churchgoers value periods of silence during the service while only 14% do not.

- Men and women hold similar views on silence.

- Introverts and extraverts hold similar views on silence before the service.

- Extraverts see more need for periods of silence during worship than introverts.

- Senior and younger churchgoers both value silence, but value it at different times.

- Senior churchgoers are more likely than younger churchgoers to value silence before the service.

- Younger churchgoers are more likely than senior churchgoers to value silence during the service.

Reflection

Much of life in today's world is filled by sounds. In many houses the radio or television is on much of the time. Periods of silence are of crucial importance. Many churchgoers value the opportunity for silence provided by the local church. Some churches deliberately develop the time before the service begins as a time for silence (or for organ music) and people are discouraged from talking to one another. Some people arrive early to benefit from this period of silence. Some churches deliberately develop periods of silence during the regular rhythm of the service, perhaps after the readings, after the sermon, or after the distribution of communion. Awkwardness about using silence may shorten these periods to no more than a second or two. When it is known that these periods of silence exist, some people practise ways of using the silence to reflect on what has been read, spoken, or experienced.

I'm pleased to say Mrs Prendergast that the PCC has just bought this new, state of the art, meditation friendly, silent vacuum cleaner!

Activity

Arrange a parish workshop to explore and to experience silence. It may be helpful to go away to a retreat centre or to somewhere with space and open grounds. It may be possible to make good use of the local church, the churchyard and so on. Include a silent meal in the course of the workshop.

Talking points

- Is there silence before the service in your church?

- Are there regular spaces for silence in the services in your church?

- Is enough use made of silence in your church?

- Are the periods of silence long enough?

- Is too much use made of silence in your church?

- Should more opportunities for silence be provided in your church?

- Who values silence most in your church?

- Who seems to value silence least in your church?

- How can the needs of those who want silence and those who do not want silence best be met?

- How can people be helped to make use of periods of silence?

19   Ways of making music

Organ music

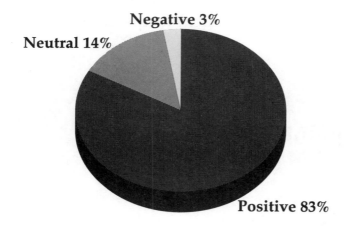

Positive 83%	
Males	82%
Females	84%
Under 50 years	78%
50-64 years	84%
Over 64 years	86%
Introverts	84%
Ambiverts	83%
Extraverts	81%

Music group

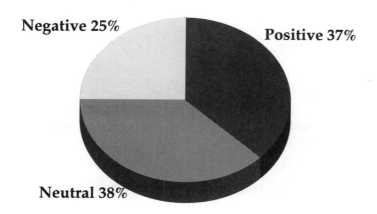

Positive 37%	
Males	38%
Females	37%
Under 50 years	50%
50-64 years	34%
Over 64 years	29%
Introverts	35%
Ambiverts	39%
Extraverts	39%

Listening to the statistics

- The majority of rural churchgoers hold a positive view of organ music in church.

- Only 3% of churchgoers do not find organ music helpful.

- Men and women hold similar attitudes toward organ music.

- Introverts and extraverts hold similar views regarding organ music.

- Younger churchgoers hold a slightly less positive view of organ music than senior churchgoers.

- Rural churchgoers are much less enthusiastic about music groups than about organ music.

- Two out of every five rural churchgoers find music groups helpful.

- Men and women hold similar attitudes towards music groups.

- Introverts are slightly less in favour of music groups than extraverts.

- Younger churchgoers are nearly twice as likely to find music groups helpful than senior churchgoers.

Reflection

Trends in church music have changed many times over the centuries. Thomas Hardy's novels, for example, provide good illustrations of the bands of local musicians who provided music in many rural churches before organs became so popular in the nineteenth century. Now the organ is often regarded as the only appropriate instrument for use in church. Traditional pipe organs and harmoniums have now been joined by electric organs. Some churches, however, make good use of local musicians to form a music group, either on a regular basis or for special or one-off occasions. Sometimes local schools are happy to provide a group of musicians for special services. Some people prefer a good piano as a better instrument for accompanying singing.

Now this is the De Guidon Crypt.... please, never sit here, as the organ rises from below at the beginning of each service.

Activity

Invite a group of local musicians to provide the music for a special service, like a carol service, harvest festival or local celebration. You may consider approaching the school orchestra, a local silver band or an informal group of friends who make music together. Involve the musicians in planning the service. From time to time try singing verses of hymns unaccompanied.

Talking points

- How is music made in your church?

- When was the present organ installed?

- What did the present organ replace and why?

- When was the first organ installed in your church?

- In what condition is your church organ?

- Who plays the organ in your church?

- On how many other organists can your church draw?

- What is your church doing to train organists for the future?

- Does your church ever make use of music groups?

- How many instrumentalists are associated with your church?

- Are there opportunities for developing music groups?

- Do local schools ever contribute music in your church?

- Are there opportunities for developing further musical links with local schools?

20   Ways of singing

Robed choir

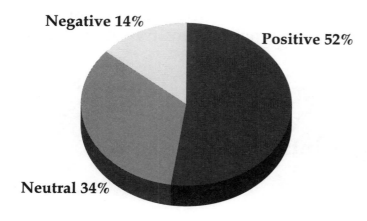

Positive 52%	
Males	57%
Females	49%
Under 50 years	42%
50-64 years	52%
Over 64 years	62%
Introverts	52%
Ambiverts	52%
Extraverts	53%

Chanted psalms

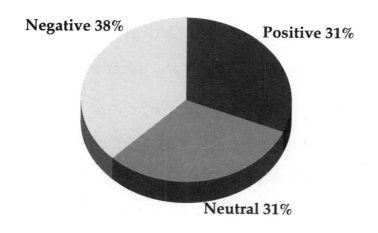

Positive 31%	
Males	33%
Females	29%
Under 50 years	19%
50-64 years	34%
Over 64 years	40%
Introverts	29%
Ambiverts	33%
Extraverts	31%

 **Listening to the statistics**

- About half of rural churchgoers find value in robed choirs.

- Men are more likely to value robed choirs than women.

- Senior churchgoers are more likely to value robed choirs than younger churchgoers.

- Introverts and extraverts hold similar views on robed choirs.

- More rural churchgoers find chanted psalms unhelpful than find them helpful.

- There is little difference in the ways in which men and women value chanted psalms.

- Introverts and extraverts hold similar views on chanted psalms.

- Senior churchgoers are twice as likely to value chanted psalms as younger churchgoers.

Reflection

The great Anglican cathedrals are well known for their musical tradition. They maintain robed choirs, professional directors of music, and a disciplined way of singing the psalms. Some of these cathedrals also maintain choir schools to guarantee a regular supply of high quality young voices. It is from these roots that the idea of a distinctively Anglican form of choral service emerged. Sometimes this tradition has transferred well to the local parish church when there has been sufficient musical talent and commitment in the local area to make it work. Sometimes this tradition has transferred less well to the local church. One of the major drawbacks of the cathedral tradition of church music is that it disenfranchises the local congregation, who may find it difficult to join in with the singing.

...and the first robed choir was introduced to this church in 1864.

Psst ... I think they're still here!

Activity

Arrange a visit to attend choral evensong in your local cathedral, but check that the choir is in residence before you go. Afterwards discuss the differences between cathedral worship and worship in the local parish church.

Talking points

- Is there a robed choir in your church?

- When was the first robed choir introduced to your church?

- Does the choir find it easy to recruit new members?

- How much money does the PCC commit to training and resourcing the choir?

- Is there any sense of division between the choir and the congregation?

- Are psalms sung in your church?

- To what system or method are psalms sung in your church?

- Who chooses the way in which psalms are sung in your church?

- Who likes singing psalms in your church?

- Who does not like singing psalms in your church?

- Which translation of the psalms is used in your church?

- Why are psalms used in church anyway?

21   Using recorded music

Playing recorded music

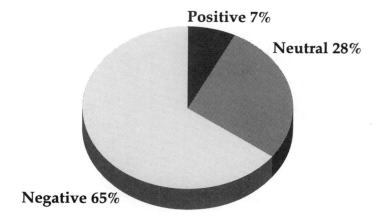

Positive 7%	
Males	7%
Females	8%
Under 50 years	11%
50-64 years	8%
Over 64 years	3%
Introverts	6%
Ambiverts	7%
Extraverts	9%

Playing recorded hymns

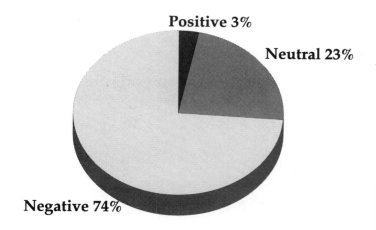

Positive 3%	
Males	3%
Females	4%
Under 50 years	5%
50-64 years	2%
Over 64 years	3%
Introverts	3%
Ambiverts	3%
Extraverts	5%

Listening to the statistics

- Very few churchgoers (only 7%) find recorded music helpful in church.

- Two out of every three churchgoers find recorded music in church positively unhelpful.

- Younger churchgoers hold a slightly more positive attitude toward recorded music than senior churchgoers.

- Only 3% of churchgoers find recorded hymn tunes helpful in church.

- Three out of every four churchgoers find recorded hymn tunes in church positively unhelpful.

- Younger churchgoers hold no more positive attitude toward recorded hymn tunes than senior churchgoers.

- Men and women hold similar attitudes to playing recorded music and hymn tunes in church.

- Introverts and extraverts hold similar attitudes to playing recorded music and hymn tunes in church.

Reflection

Some churches find it increasingly difficult to find a musician to accompany the hymns or to provide appropriate music before and after the service. One solution to this problem is to use prerecorded music. Several firms now market series of prerecorded hymn tunes for use in local churches. Some of these recordings also include a vocal accompaniment. For prerecorded music to be used to good effect it is essential that an adequate sound system should be available. Well selected prerecorded music can also contribute to the atmosphere if played before and after the service, or at appropriate points during the service, like the distribution of communion.

And now we are going to meditate
with the aid of some choral music
recorded on the 'Our Master's Voice' label.

Activity

Arrange an evening of 'Excerpts from your favourite records' in church. Make every effort to obtain an appropriate sound system. Perhaps a local music shop would be willing to loan a sound system as part of a promotional campaign. Invite local people to nominate extracts of music (and to provide them on disk, tape or CD). Draw up a programme and promote it in the local community.

Talking points

- Does your church ever experience difficulty in finding a musician to accompany the hymns?

- Has your church ever tried using prerecorded music?

- What is the attitude toward using prerecorded music in your church?

- Are there occasions when it would be helpful to experiment with prerecorded music in your church?

- Is your church ever open for special events (like a flower festival) when prerecorded music would add to the atmosphere?

- Does your church possess an adequate sound system to make good use of prerecorded music?

22   Welcoming worshippers

Being greeted as you leave

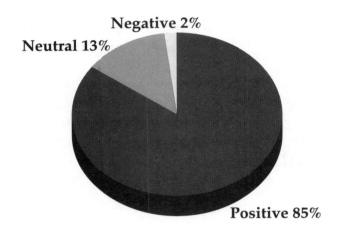

Positive 85%	
Males	84%
Females	86%
Under 50 years	86%
50-64 years	85%
Over 64 years	85%
Introverts	86%
Ambiverts	83%
Extraverts	88%

Warm welcome on arrival

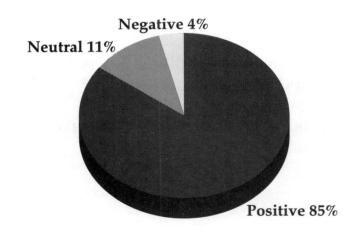

Positive 85%	
Males	85%
Females	86%
Under 50 years	87%
50-64 years	84%
Over 64 years	86%
Introverts	86%
Ambiverts	84%
Extraverts	88%

 # Listening to the statistics

- The majority of churchgoers appreciate being greeted when they arrive and leave church.

- Only four in every hundred churchgoers feel put off by a warm welcome on arrival.

- Only two in every hundred churchgoers feel put off by being greeted as they leave.

- Men and women feel equally positive about being greeted as they arrive and leave church.

- Younger and senior churchgoers feel equally positive about being greeted as they arrive and leave church.

- Introverts and extraverts feel equally positive about being greeted as they arrive and leave church.

Reflection

Churches vary very much regarding the way in which they treat people as they arrive and leave. In some places there is always someone by the door to greet the worshippers and to help visitors or newcomers find their books and somewhere to sit. In other places visitors and newcomers are left to find their own way. Practices differ in a similar way after the service. In some places people drift away very quickly, hardly speaking to each other. In some places groups of people who know each other form tightly knit groups which exclude other people. In some places an attempt is made to greet everyone. Some clergy make a habit of standing by the door to speak to everyone as they go. In today's rural church, however, the priest is often on his or her way to take another service in a neighbouring church long before everyone has left.

We thought it would be a good idea
to help people get to know each other.

Activity

Arrange for a number of the members of the church to attend services in other churches, to go as visitors either alone or in pairs. Ask them to give particular attention to the kind of welcome they receive and how they felt about their arrival and departure from that church. Then provide an opportunity for the experiences to be shared, discussed and evaluated.

Talking points

- What happens in your church to welcome people as they arrive?

- What happens in your church to make contact with people as they leave?

- Who takes responsibility for helping visitors and newcomers to feel at home?

- Is enough being done in your church to make people feel welcome?

- Are your local clergy able to meet people after the service or are they needed to take services elsewhere?

- Who particularly likes being greeted in your church?

- Are there some people in your church who prefer not to be greeted and welcomed?

- Do you know the name of everybody who attends your church?

23   Social encounter

Chance to chat before the service

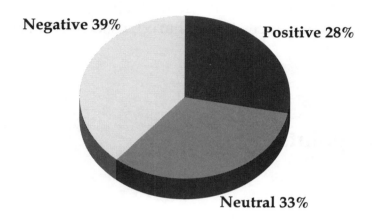

Positive 28%	
Males	25%
Females	28%
Under 50 years	33%
50-64 years	23%
Over 64 years	25%
Introverts	25%
Ambiverts	28%
Extraverts	28%

Refreshments afterwards

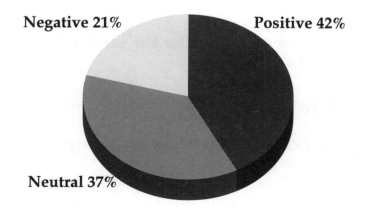

Positive 42%	
Males	46%
Females	40%
Under 50 years	54%
50-64 years	40%
Over 64 years	37%
Introverts	44%
Ambiverts	41%
Extraverts	42%

Listening to the statistics

- Considerably more churchgoers find the chance to chat before the service unhelpful than find it helpful.

- Twice as many churchgoers find refreshments after the service helpful than find them unhelpful.

- Two out of every five churchgoers dislike chatting before the service.

- One in every five churchgoers dislike refreshments after the service.

- Men and women hold similar attitudes towards chatting before the service.

- Men value refreshments after the service more than women.

- Younger churchgoers are more inclined to want to chat before the service than older churchgoers.

- Younger churchgoers are more inclined to value refreshments after the service than older churchgoers.

- Introverts and extraverts hold similar views on chatting before the service and on refreshments after the service.

Reflection

There are two clearly opposing views on the social context of attending church services. Some people see going to church as an opportunity to meet and talk with their friends. Other people prefer to make a clear distinction between attending church services and going out for a social event. It is for this reason that chatting before the service and refreshments after the service can be controversial issues in some churches. Chatting before the service can be in direct opposition to the preference expressed by some people for silence before the service (see section 13). If refreshments are provided after the service those who wish to stay may do so, while those who do not wish to stay may slip away. If refreshments are to be provided after the service, there needs to be a way of doing so without disrupting the service, for example with a noisy urn in the back pew.

VESTRY BAR

Activity

Take a careful look at the facilities your church has for providing refreshments after the service. In what condition is the kettle or urn? How inviting are the cups? How adequate are the kitchen facilities? Is the best use made of the environment for serving and drinking coffee? Is there potential for tables, chairs and a comfortable area for drinking coffee? Try experimenting with improving these facilities.

Talking points

- Do people chat before the service in your church?

- Are there people who dislike chatting before the service begins?

- How can these two groups of people be reconciled?

- Are refreshments available after the service in your church?

- Who wants to stay for refreshments?

- Who does not want to stay for refreshments?

- When refreshments are provided who is responsible for them?

- Is your church adequately resourced for providing refreshments?

- How could you make refreshments after the service more attractive and more welcoming?

24   Ways of teaching

A sermon

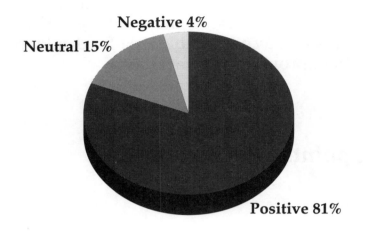

Positive 81%	
Males	81%
Females	82%
Under 50 years	78%
50-64 years	80%
Over 64 years	86%
Introverts	87%
Ambiverts	79%
Extraverts	80%

Discussion in the services

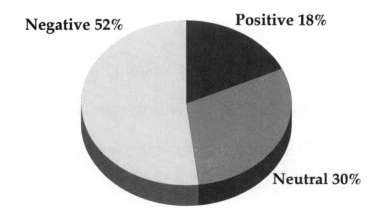

Positive 18%	
Males	18%
Females	18%
Under 50 years	24%
50-64 years	19%
Over 64 years	12%
Introverts	14%
Ambiverts	18%
Extraverts	23%

Listening to the statistics

- The vast majority of churchgoers (81%) find sermons a positive experience.

- Men and women hold an equally positive view of sermons.

- Younger churchgoers hold a slightly less positive attitude toward sermons than senior churchgoers.

- Extraverts hold a slightly less positive attitude toward sermons than introverts.

- Less than one in five churchgoers (18%) find discussion in services a positive experience.

- Men and women hold an equally negative view of discussion in services.

- Introverts hold a more negative view of discussion in services than extraverts.

- Senior churchgoers hold a more negative view of discussion in services than younger churchgoers.

Reflection

The Anglican church claims to be both Catholic and Reformed. In the Catholic tradition the sacrament is central; in the Reformed tradition preaching is central. Falling between the two traditions Anglicanism can both appear to value and to undervalue the sermon. In former days the services of matins and evensong often provided good opportunities for preaching. Today the family communion service favours short sermons. This raises two key questions. Are Anglican churchgoers now offered enough teaching? Is the sermon the most appropriate method of teaching for the twenty-first century? Alternatives to preaching include involving the congregation in more interactive teaching methods, of which discussion techniques provide a good example.

You have just three minutes before you must stop writing...

Activity

Invite members of the congregation to take notes during the sermon and:
    to highlight one phrase or idea they found interesting;
    to raise one point for further information;
    to choose one issue for debate.

Talking points

- How many sermons are preached in your church in a year?

- How long is the average sermon in your church?

- On what themes have recent sermons been given in your church?

- What do you remember most about sermons?

- How much do you remember about the sermon last Sunday?

- What would you miss most if sermons were replaced by a different teaching method in your church?

- Is discussion ever used in your church as an alternative teaching method?

- Who would respond well to discussion in the services in your church?

- Who would not like discussion in the services in your church?

25   Reverence and humour

Reverence

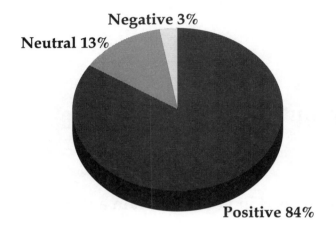

Positive 84%	
Males	82%
Females	85%
Under 50 years	75%
50-64 years	85%
Over 64 years	92%
Introverts	89%
Ambiverts	81%
Extraverts	82%

Fun and humour

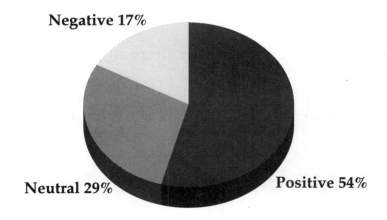

Positive 54%	
Males	51%
Females	55%
Under 50 years	71%
50-64 years	51%
Over 64 years	38%
Introverts	47%
Ambiverts	53%
Extraverts	58%

Listening to the statistics

- The majority of churchgoers (84%) find reverence an important part of worship.

- Men and women hold similar views on reverence.

- Younger churchgoers place less value on reverence than senior churchgoers.

- Introverts place a higher value on reverence than extraverts.

- Many more churchgoers value fun and humour in worship than are put off by fun and humour.

- Just over half of churchgoers find fun and humour contributes to their appreciation of worship.

- Younger churchgoers are twice as likely to value fun and humour in worship as senior churchgoers.

- Extraverts are more likely to value fun and humour in worship than introverts.

- Women are slightly more likely to value fun and humour in worship than men.

Reflection

Many people feel that good worship should be characterised by reverence. To many people reverence means taking worship seriously, treating worship as special, and having worship well planned, ordered and presented. Reverence does not imply being glum, overly pious, or humourless. In good worship there is room not only for reverence, but for fun and humour as well. Fun and humour is able to catch the attention, focus the concentration, and communicate the difficult or uncomfortable message. The younger generation especially, who have grown up in the age of the professional television presenter, expects worship to be presented with equal professionalism. The key is to find the right mixture between reverence and humour.

Activity

Make a collection of books of religious humour and religious cartoons. Collect cartoons from the church press. Make some enlarged photocopies of the cartoons to display, or copy them on to overhead projector sheets. Encourage a debate about good taste and bad taste in religious humour and about the place of humour in church.

Talking points

- What are the main signs of reverence in your services?

- How do the leaders of your services communicate a sense of reverence?

- When have you felt reverence to be lost in your church?

- What helps your sense of reverence in church?

- What place has fun and humour in your church?

- Who appreciates fun and humour in your church?

- Who disapproves of fun and humour in your church?

- How can those who like fun and humour and those who do not like fun and humour be reconciled?

- What recent examples of fun and humour do you recall in your church?

26   Dance and drama

Drama in the service

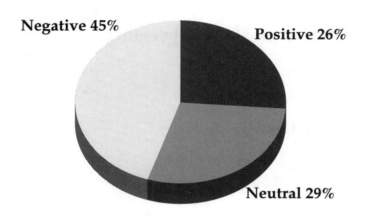

Positive 26%	
Males	25%
Females	26%
Under 50 years	43%
50-64 years	22%
Over 64 years	13%
Introverts	24%
Ambiverts	26%
Extraverts	27%

Dance in the service

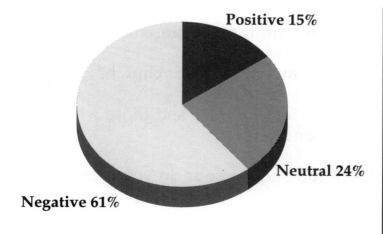

Positive 15%	
Males	13%
Females	16%
Under 50 years	25%
50-64 years	13%
Over 64 years	7%
Introverts	15%
Ambiverts	12%
Extraverts	17%

 # Listening to the statistics

- Nearly twice as many churchgoers find drama in services unhelpful as find it helpful.

- Four times as many churchgoers find dance in services unhelpful as find it helpful.

- One in four churchgoers find drama helpful in services.

- One in seven churchgoers find dance helpful in services.

- Men and women hold similar views on dance and drama in services.

- Younger churchgoers are considerably more open to dance and drama in services than senior churchgoers.

- Introverts and extraverts hold similar views on dance and drama in services.

Reflection

Dance and drama can provide very powerful ways of communicating both ideas and emotions. It is not surprising, therefore, that dance and drama have a proper place within the worship of the church. Sometimes a short piece of improvised drama can contribute greatly to the power and effect of a sermon. Sometimes a whole sermon can be replaced by a carefully presented excerpt from a play, like Eliot's *Murder in the Cathedral*. Sometimes drama enables a range of individuals to become involved in the ministry of the church who would never dream of becoming involved in other ways. Sometimes liturgical dance can enable individuals to give expression to their faith and commitment in ways which they are unable to do through words. The artistic expression conveyed through dance or drama can uplift the soul.

Alas poor Moses, I knew him well...

Activity

Arrange for dance or drama to have a special place in a service. Consider inviting a liturgical dance group from another church or from a neighbouring college or university. Consider inviting a local drama society to present an excerpt from an appropriate play. Consider inviting a local school to present drama in the service.

Talking points

- When has drama been used in services in your church?

- When could drama be used in services in your church?

- Who are the individuals who would like to contribute to drama in your services?

- Who are the individuals who may disapprove of drama in your services?

- When has dance been used in services in your church?

- On which special occasions might dance be used in services in your church?

- Who are the individuals who would like to contribute to dance in your services?

- Who are the individuals who may disapprove of dance in your services?

- Are there people in the local community, who do not generally attend church, who may like to contribute to dance or drama in your services?

27   Communication

Pew leaflets

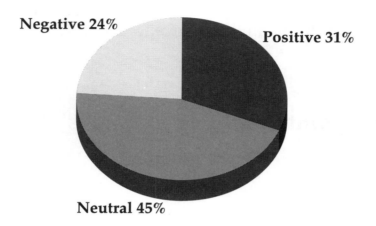

Negative 24%

Positive 31%

Neutral 45%

Positive 31%	
Males	34%
Females	28%
Under 50 years	29%
50-64 years	31%
Over 64 years	32%
Introverts	28%
Ambiverts	34%
Extraverts	29%

Page numbers announced

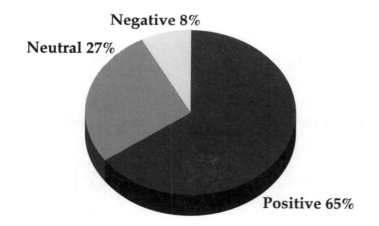

Negative 8%

Neutral 27%

Positive 65%

Positive 65%	
Males	62%
Females	67%
Under 50 years	60%
50-64 years	65%
Over 64 years	69%
Introverts	67%
Ambiverts	62%
Extraverts	66%

Listening to the statistics

- Only one in three churchgoers find pew leaflets helpful.

- One in four churchgoers find pew leaflets a distraction.

- Men have a more positive view of pew leaflets than women.

- Younger and senior churchgoers hold similar views on pew leaflets.

- Two in three churchgoers find it helpful to have page numbers announced.

- Less than one in ten churchgoers find having page numbers announced a distraction.

- Men have a slightly less positive view of having page numbers announced than women.

- Younger churchgoers have a slightly less positive view of having page numbers announced than senior churchgoers.

- Introverts and extraverts hold similar views on pew leaflets and on having page numbers announced.

Reflection

Anglican services are often heavily dependent on using service books. It would be a mistake to think that even all regular churchgoers really know their way around these books. Visitors to Anglican services may experience even greater difficulty. For example, visitors to a rite A communion service using *The Alternative Service Book 1980* may be surprised to find that the service begins on page 119, that the confession is printed in two different places and that, if the first eucharistic prayer is used, three other eucharistic prayers intervene before the Lord's Prayer is printed, and then the Lord's Prayer is printed in two versions. Some churches try to help by printing a guideline to the order of service. Some visitors may find juggling with this extra leaflet even more confusing. Some churches make a careful point of announcing page numbers as the service goes on.

We will now sing
hymn 396,
the three hundred and ninety-sixth hymn.
Number 3 - 9 - 6
on page 645
in the large red hymn books....

Activity

Make a collection and display of pew leaflets produced by different churches. Compare the different styles and evaluate their usefulness. Try designing experimental pew leaflets for your own church.

Talking points

• How well do your regular churchgoers know their way through the service book?

• How well are visitors able to follow the order of service in your church?

• Does your church provide a pew leaflet with information about how to follow the service?

• Are page numbers given out in your church sufficiently to help the visitor?

• Are there individuals who dislike page numbers being given out in your services?

• Whose responsibility is it to help visitors follow the service?

• Do you think your church needs to revise its policy about providing pew leaflets or announcing page numbers?

28   Lay leadership

Service led by clergy

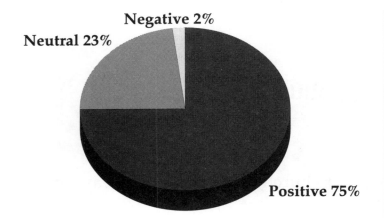

Positive 75%	
Males	76%
Females	75%
Under 50 years	68%
50-64 years	74%
Over 64 years	83%
Introverts	78%
Ambiverts	73%
Extraverts	74%

Service led by laity

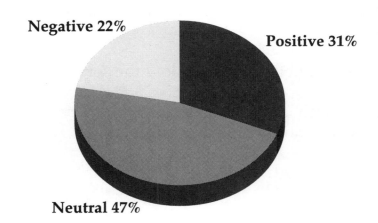

Positive 31%	
Males	32%
Females	30%
Under 50 years	33%
50-64 years	29%
Over 64 years	30%
Introverts	29%
Ambiverts	32%
Extraverts	32%

 # Listening to the statistics

- The majority of churchgoers have a positive attitude towards clergy leading services.

- Just 2% of churchgoers feel that services are spoilt by having clergy lead them.

- Less than a third of churchgoers have a positive attitude toward laity leading services.

- Nearly a quarter of churchgoers feel that services are spoilt by having laity lead them.

- Younger churchgoers have a less positive attitude toward clergy leading services than senior churchgoers.

- Younger and senior churchgoers hold similar views on laity leading services.

- Introverts have a slightly more positive attitude toward clergy leading services than extraverts.

- Introverts and extraverts hold similar views on laity leading services.

- Men and women hold similar views to having services led by clergy or by laity.

Reflection

Anglicanism has been, until recently, a clerically dominated denomination. Clergy have taken the services, read the lessons and preached the sermons. More recently two factors have stimulated a greater involvement of the laity in the leadership of worship. The first factor has been a *theological* shift in the rediscovery of the ministry of the laity. Theologically, it is argued, baptism equips all Christians for ministry. The second factor has been a *practical* consequence of the rapid decline in the number of clergy, especially among those serving in rural dioceses. Churches have been encouraged to challenge local people to accept new roles in ministry. Some dioceses have organised training programmes for laity. Some dioceses have introduced recognised titles for lay ministers, like elders or pastoral assistants, with or without specific training requirements.

Well dear, I do not have to get up, everybody else is leading the service.

Activity

Find out about the wide variety of lay ministry practised in different dioceses, in different denominations, and in different local churches. Produce a poster display on lay ministry. Invite someone from the diocese to speak about the development of lay ministry within the diocese. Then consider the range of talents in the congregation and community which are not currently expressed in the worship of your church.

Talking points

• Do lay people read lessons in your church?

• Do lay people act as eucharistic assistants in your church?

• Do lay people lead the intercessions in your church?

• Do lay people lead the service (or part of the service) in your church?

• Do lay people preach in your church?

• How often are services led by laity in the absence of clergy in your church?

• What is the attitude toward lay leadership of services in your church?

• What is done in your church to challenge and to train lay people for leadership in services?

29   Deploying ministers

Variety of preachers

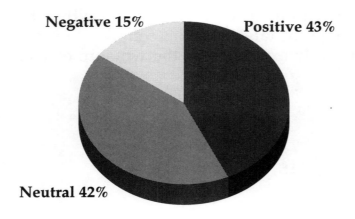

Positive 43%	
Males	48%
Females	41%
Under 50 years	47%
50-64 years	47%
Over 64 years	38%
Introverts	48%
Ambiverts	45%
Extraverts	38%

Same minister each week

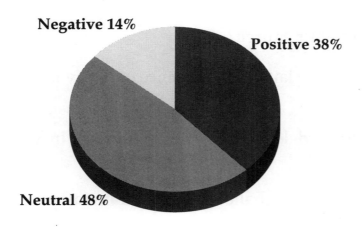

Positive 38%	
Males	37%
Females	40%
Under 50 years	37%
50-64 years	39%
Over 64 years	39%
Introverts	39%
Ambiverts	38%
Extraverts	40%

 # Listening to the statistics

- Nearly three times as many churchgoers find a variety of preachers helpful as find it unhelpful.

- Two fifths of churchgoers say they like a variety of preachers.

- Men are more likely to appreciate a variety of preachers than women.

- Younger churchgoers are more likely to appreciate a variety of preachers than senior churchgoers.

- Introverts are more likely to appreciate a variety of preachers than extraverts.

- Nearly three times as many churchgoers find having the same minister each week helpful as find it unhelpful.

- The largest proportion of churchgoers are not bothered whether they have the same minister each week or not.

- Neither gender nor age influence attitudes toward having the same minister each week.

- Introverts and extraverts hold similar attitudes toward having the same minister each week.

Reflection

In the recent past the vast majority of rural churches had their own parson and *he* was responsible for taking nearly all the services, week in and week out. In some cases this led to a close relationship between priest and people. In some cases it led to empty churches. In today's rural church the old pattern has all but broken down. In multi-parish benefices the one priest is responsible for many churches. In some areas several clergy work together as a group or team ministry covering a large number of churches. Readers and other lay people are of increasing importance in keeping the pattern of services and preaching going. For some people this has added a richness and variety to the Sunday services. For other people it has indicated the impersonalisation of the rural church and a growing distance between the priest and the local community.

VICARS OF ST EDITHS

Cedric Flood 1901–1961
John Snore   1962–

Activity

Look into the history of your local church. Display the names (and photographs) of the vicars or rectors over the past hundred years, showing the year when they came to the parish and the year when they left. Note how many churches for which they were responsible (and how many curates they had). Draw up a list of the ways in which ministry changes with a shift to multi-parish rural benefices. Invite your priest to analyse a typical week's work and to share this on a poster.

Talking points

- How many different preachers gave sermons in your church last year?

- What are the advantages of a variety of preachers?

- What are the disadvantages of a variety of preachers?

- Would you prefer more or fewer preachers in your church?

- How many different people lead services in your church?

- Would you prefer more or fewer ministers taking services in your church?

- What are the advantages of having the same minister every week?

- What are the disadvantages of having the same minister every week?

30   Dressing the clergy

Robed ministers

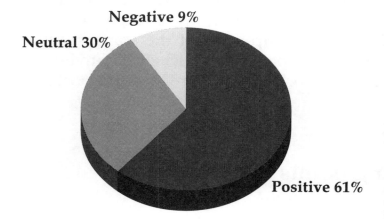

Positive 61%	
Males	65%
Females	58%
Under 50 years	45%
50-64 years	65%
Over 64 years	71%
Introverts	62%
Ambiverts	59%
Extraverts	62%

Full vestments

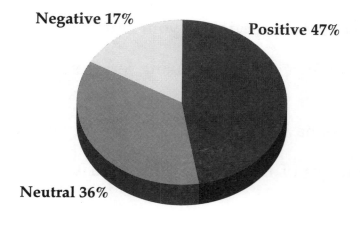

Positive 47%	
Males	48%
Females	48%
Under 50 years	38%
50-64 years	52%
Over 64 years	54%
Introverts	45%
Ambiverts	48%
Extraverts	51%

Listening to the statistics

- Seven times as many churchgoers find having ministers robed an aid to worship as find it a distraction.

- One in ten churchgoers would prefer clergy not to be robed.

- Men are more positive about having ministers robed than women.

- Younger churchgoers are much less positive about having ministers robed than senior churchgoers.

- Introverts and extraverts hold similar views on robed ministers.

- Many more churchgoers have a positive attitude toward full vestments than have a negative attitude toward full vestments.

- Less than a fifth of churchgoers are put off by full vestments.

- Men and women hold similar views on full vestments.

- Younger churchgoers are much less positive about full vestments than senior churchgoers.

- Introverts are less positive about full vestments than extraverts.

Reflection

Like so many other aspects of church life, fashion in clerical dress has a varied history in the Anglican church. In the nineteenth century the great divide between the Tractarian (high church) and the Evangelical (low church) movements was clearly reflected in what the clergy wore. High churchmen wore full vestments. Low churchmen wore surplice, hood and scarf. These traditions in dress persist in many village churches, although the *theological* reasons behind the local custom may well have been forgotten. It is, anyway, much less easy to keep up ancient divisions of churchmanship in contemporary multi-parish rural benefices. Indeed, some churches today have abandoned clerical robes altogether and prefer to see the ministers lead services dressed in their everyday clothes.

Activity

Collect and display pictures of clergy robed according to a number of different church traditions. Try to include Free Church, Catholic and Orthodox clergy as well as Anglicans. Discuss what these vestments say about the different clergy and about their traditions. What is the origin and significance of the different robes?

Talking points

- What do the clergy wear to take services in your church?

- Does your church possess a full set of vestments in the various liturgical colours?

- When were these vestments acquired and what condition are they in?

- When was the present pattern of clerical dress established in your church and why?

- Are services ever led in your church by ministers wearing their everyday clothes?

- Who looks after the robes and vestments in your church?

- Are any robes or vestments in need of repair, replacement, or better storage conditions?

- Is everyone in your church content with the present practice of 'dressing the clergy'?

Appendix

The questionnaire

PART ONE How do the following components contribute towards your experience of good worship? Please assess each issue by drawing a circle round one number between 1 and 5.

1 means very negative   3 means neutral   5 means very positive

Silence before the service	1 2 3 4 5	Bible teaching	1 2 3 4 5
Good music before the service	1 2 3 4 5	Service led by clergy	1 2 3 4 5
Chance to chat before the service	1 2 3 4 5	Service led by laity	1 2 3 4 5
Traditional church architecture	1 2 3 4 5	Service led by men	1 2 3 4 5
Modern church building	1 2 3 4 5	Service led by women	1 2 3 4 5
Warm welcome on arrival	1 2 3 4 5	Service led by a team	1 2 3 4 5
Sharing the peace	1 2 3 4 5	Same minister each week	1 2 3 4 5
Being greeted as you leave	1 2 3 4 5	Different ministers each week	1 2 3 4 5
Refreshments afterwards	1 2 3 4 5	Variety of preachers	1 2 3 4 5
Congregation spread out	1 2 3 4 5	Robed ministers	1 2 3 4 5
Congregation sitting together	1 2 3 4 5	Full vestments	1 2 3 4 5
Traditional pews	1 2 3 4 5	Nave altar	1 2 3 4 5
Modern chairs	1 2 3 4 5	Clergy facing the people	1 2 3 4 5
Candles on altar	1 2 3 4 5	Clergy facing the altar	1 2 3 4 5
Incense	1 2 3 4 5	Robed choir	1 2 3 4 5
Pew leaflets	1 2 3 4 5	Music group	1 2 3 4 5
Enough bibles for everyone	1 2 3 4 5	Organ music	1 2 3 4 5
Enough service books for all	1 2 3 4 5	Playing recorded music	1 2 3 4 5
Service books in good condition	1 2 3 4 5	Playing recorded hymns	1 2 3 4 5
Traditional hymns	1 2 3 4 5	Traditional bible translations	1 2 3 4 5
Modern hymns	1 2 3 4 5	Modern bible translations	1 2 3 4 5
Gospel songs	1 2 3 4 5	Readings from non biblical books	1 2 3 4 5
Choruses	1 2 3 4 5	Drama in the service	1 2 3 4 5
Chanted psalms	1 2 3 4 5	Dance in the service	1 2 3 4 5
Said psalms	1 2 3 4 5	Discussion in the service	1 2 3 4 5
Well read lessons	1 2 3 4 5	Fun and humour	1 2 3 4 5
1662 Book of Common Prayer	1 2 3 4 5	Reverence	1 2 3 4 5
Alternative Service Book 1980	1 2 3 4 5	Sense of mystery	1 2 3 4 5
Holy communion	1 2 3 4 5	Children present for the service	1 2 3 4 5
Matins	1 2 3 4 5	Crèche facilities	1 2 3 4 5
Evensong	1 2 3 4 5	Good sound system	1 2 3 4 5
Family services	1 2 3 4 5	Good lighting system	1 2 3 4 5
Songs of praise	1 2 3 4 5	Good heating system	1 2 3 4 5
Informal services	1 2 3 4 5	Access for the disabled	1 2 3 4 5
Extempore prayer	1 2 3 4 5	Loop system for hard of hearing	1 2 3 4 5
Speaking in tongues	1 2 3 4 5	Large print for partially sighted	1 2 3 4 5
Periods of silence	1 2 3 4 5	Comfortable seating	1 2 3 4 5
Page numbers announced	1 2 3 4 5	Comfortable kneelers	1 2 3 4 5
A sermon	1 2 3 4 5	Toilet available	1 2 3 4 5

PART TWO Please provide information about yourself by ticking the appropriate boxes.

Age group

under 20	1	
20 - 34	2	
35 - 49	3	
50 - 64	4	
65 and over	5	

Sex

male	1	
female	2	

Denomination

none	1	
Church of England	2	
Roman Catholic	3	
Free Church	4	
other (specify)	5	

Church attendance

weekly	4	
at least monthly	3	
sometimes	2	
never	1	

Where you normally worship

village	4	
market town	3	
urban	2	
suburban	1	

Personal prayer

daily	4	
at least weekly	3	
sometimes	2	
never	1	

Please answer the following questions by putting a circle around the 'YES' or the 'NO'. Do not think too long about the exact meaning of the questions.

Does your mood often go up and down? .... YES NO
Are you a talkative person? .... YES NO
Would being in debt worry you? .... YES NO
Are you rather lively? .... YES NO
Were you ever greedy by helping yourself to more than your share of anything?.............. YES NO
Would you take drugs which may have strange or dangerous effects? .... YES NO
Have you ever blamed someone for doing something you knew was really your fault? ... YES NO
Do you prefer to go your own way rather than act by the rules? .... YES NO
Do you often feel 'fed-up'? .... YES NO
Have you ever taken anything (even a pin or button) that belonged to someone else? ...... YES NO
Would you call yourself a nervous person? .... YES NO
Do you think marriage is old-fashioned and should be done away with? .... YES NO
Can you easily get some life into a rather dull party? .... YES NO
Are you a worrier? .... YES NO
Do you tend to keep in the background on social occasions? .... YES NO
Does it worry you if you know there are mistakes in your work? .... YES NO
Have you ever cheated at a game? .... YES NO
Do you suffer from 'nerves'? .... YES NO
Have you ever taken advantage of someone? .... YES NO
Are you mostly quiet when you are with other people? .... YES NO
Do you often feel lonely? .... YES NO
Is it better to follow society's rules than go your own way? .... YES NO
Do other people think of you as being very lively? .... YES NO
Do you always practise what you preach? .... YES NO